Jane Menzies

# Cynewulf's Elene

A metrical translation from Zupitza's edition

Jane Menzies

**Cynewulf's Elene**
*A metrical translation from Zupitza's edition*

ISBN/EAN: 9783741112973

Manufactured in Europe, USA, Canada, Australia, Japa

Cover: Foto ©Andreas Hilbeck / pixelio.de

Manufactured and distributed by brebook publishing software
(www.brebook.com)

Jane Menzies

**Cynewulf´s Elene**

# CYNEWULF'S 'ELENE'

ST HELENA, THE MOTHER OF CONSTANTINE.

# CYNEWULF'S 'ELENE'

*A METRICAL TRANSLATION FROM*
*ZUPITZA'S EDITION*

BY

JANE MENZIES

WILLIAM BLACKWOOD AND SONS
EDINBURGH AND LONDON
MDCCCXCV

# INTRODUCTION.

THE poem of 'Elene,' or 'The Invention of the Cross,' dates in all probability from the eighth century. Its source is by some critics supposed to be the Latin Life of Saint Cyriacus, the Judas of the poem. Others are of opinion that it came to England in Greek form. The story is briefly as follows :—

In the year 233, the sixth of the reign of Constantine, the Roman empire was overrun by Huns, Hreðgoths, and Franks. The Romans, though well prepared, are inferior in numbers. The Emperor, in a dream, sees in the clouds a shining cross with the inscription, "In hoc signo vinces." The next morning he orders a standard with a similar cross to be prepared, and borne in front of his army.

After gaining the victory, he is baptised by Sylvester, and having in vain made inquiries as to whence the vision came, he requests Helena, his mother, to sail to Palestine, and there find the true cross buried in the earth. Helena at once departs thither by sea, and arrives in Jerusalem.

She there questions the wisest Jews, without result. Judas,. one of the most sagacious of them, tells his friends in private that his father and grandfather had declared that, as soon as the cross of the Lord should be sought for, the Jewish kingdom would perish.

Helena questions Judas in vain; and not until he has been starved in a dungeon for seven days will he reveal what he knows. Brought out of his prison, he engages in prayer, and the three crosses are found. Still it is uncertain which of the three is the true cross of the Lord; and this is only determined by the restoration to life of a dead youth on whose body the true cross is laid. The devil appears, and complains of being defrauded of his rights; but Judas silences him. A joyful message is sent to Rome; and by order of Constantine, a church is erected on the spot where the cross was found. Judas is baptised, and, under the new name of Cyriacus, becomes Bishop of Jerusalem. Afterwards, by the wish of Helena, the nails which had pierced the hands and feet of the Crucified One are also found, and worked into a bit for the bridle of Constantine's war-horse. Lastly, Helena assembles the Jewish people, and exhorts them every year to celebrate the glorious day on which the Holy Cross was found. In six days summer would begin;[1] the cross was found on the 3d of May.[2]

---

[1] See note on p. 14.

[2] Though in such a tale some may expect to find symbolic truth rather

With regard to the authorship of the poem, it was discovered by Grimm that the name of "Cynewulf" is embedded in runes in the last canto. Kemble, Wright, Thorpe, and other critics, agree with Grimm in supposing him to have been the Abbot of Peterborough of that name, who lived in the eleventh century.

The critics Dietrich and Leo, however, conclude—the one from textual, the other from linguistic evidence—that Cynewulf was a poet of the eighth century. Dietrich supposes Cynewulf, in line 1277 of 'Elene,' to regret the composition of his 'Riddles,' and adds: "From the 'Riddles' it is evident that Cynewulf in his earlier years led a worldly life, taking pleasure in battle and in arms, in music and various amusements."

Dietrich ascribes to Cynewulf the "Dream of the Holy Rood," a verse of which is carved in runes on the cross at Ruthwell in Dumfriesshire. Since that cross must have been erected about the year 764, he thinks it probable that it was placed there at the command of some noble lord of that region, as a memorial to the poet Cynewulf, then an

than fact, yet the following facts are important in connection with it. Grimm tells us that it was not the Huns, but Maxentius, who crossed the Danube to attack Rome, and the battle was at Pons Albinus (Tiber). At the place where the cross lay under the earth, the heathens had erected a temple of Venus, in order to prevent the Christians from digging there,—a circumstance which the Anglo-Saxon poet conceals. After Cyriacus has found the nails and given them to Helena, she gives them to Constantine. (See Grimm's Introduction to 'Andreas and Elene.')

old man. In this supposition Grein and Ten Brink agree, and their theories together would furnish as good materials for a memoir as many modern biographers have had.

Cynewulf, by their account, was born of a noble family in the beginning of the eighth century. According to the custom of the time, though not destined for monastic orders, he was sent to a monastery school. His happy youth and early manhood are described in the Rhyme-song, and during this cheerful period the 'Riddles' were probably composed. But the days of joy and youth passed by. Cynewulf took holy orders, and began to write sacred poetry. Raised to a bishopric in 740, this promotion, in unquiet times, brought him only care and trouble. Having, without any fault of his own, provoked the anger of the Northumbrian king, he spent some time in prison, comforted and refreshed only by the writing of his poems, till, bent with age and weary of life, he resigned his office in 780, and died three or four years later in retirement.

And whither did he retire? To Ruthwell. One of his predecessors had during his own life caused a sculptured cross to be erected as a memorial of himself, and it appears not improbable that Cynewulf, on his resignation, retired to the place of his birth, where his noble ancestors had owned the land, and having chosen his tomb, caused a cross to be erected there, with verses from one of his own poems; the more likely, since in the Rhyme-song he says that fate had ordained that he should dig his own grave.

Could we be sure indeed that the fragment in the Exeter book named "The Ruined Castle" is Cynewulf's, we could then trace the various steps in his history more clearly still. The Anglo-Saxon Chronicle tells us that Northumbria was laid waste by Ethelbald in 737, three years before the time when Cynewulf became a bishop. The paternal castle of Cynewulf at Ruthwell would certainly be destroyed during this raid, so that to become a bishop was the only means of soothing his grief. Spending the last years of his life near the ruins of his ancestral halls, he sang in that poem of the transitory nature of earthly things.

That poem was the "Dream of the Holy Rood," found in the Vercelli Codex in 1832, along with 'Elene' and other poems ascribed to Cynewulf. One of these poems, the 'Elene,' and two in the Exeter book—namely, "Christ" and "Juliana"—have the name Cynewulf embedded in runic letters, which marks them out clearly as his.

But is the "Dream of the Rood" his also? Dietrich and Ten Brink have made of Cynewulf a kind of eighth-century Bacon, to whom every good production of that period must unfailingly be ascribed. In 'Elene' he writes of the Cross, and because the "Dream of the Rood" is on the same subject, it must needs be by Cynewulf also. When we try to realise how fresh and how enthralling a subject Christianity then was to the minds of men, it is not difficult to admit that even in that dark period two or even more may have written poetry about the Cross. The internal evidence adduced by Wülker in his 'Grundriss,'[1] from the "Dream of the Rood" itself, is worthy of consideration, and makes us hesitate before we assign to Cynewulf the words carved on that time-hallowed monument, which has now been placed in *replica* in four cities of the realm, and has thus brought nearer to us the art and the religion of over a thousand years ago.

Translations of 'Elene' have been made by Kemble in his 'Poetry of the Codex Vercellensis,' and by Dr Garnett of Boston. The first of these is literal, the second is also metrical. There is also a metrical translation into German by Grein; and Dr Weymouth's English prose version has valuable notes. In the present translation, rhyme and alliteration have been employed, and by frequent change of rhythm and the use of modern idiom, the translator has aimed at an attractive rendering. The text of the original has, however, been closely adhered to throughout.

The edition of Zupitza has been followed, and the various collations which it gives from other authors have been carefully considered. For the runes, Mr Gollancz's able "Excursus," appended to his artistic translation of Cynewulf's 'Christ,' and his kind revision for these pages, have been found invaluable.

To the Rev. Professor W. W. Skeat the warmest thanks are due for many useful hints, and for valuable counsels most kindly given during the final stages of the work.

[1] See Wülker's 'Grundriss,' iii. §§ 116, 117.

The frontispiece represents a bronze statue of St Helena, which stands facing the altar, near the west door of Bonn Cathedral, of which structure St Helena was the founder. The statue was cast at Rome in 1756.

J. MENZIES.

EDINBURGH, *December* 1894.

# NOTE.

Mr Gollancz's interpretation of the runes is as follows :—

ᚻ = C.    *Cene*, bold, or a warrior.

ᛰ = Y.    *Yfel*, afflicted.

ᚾ = N.    *Nÿd*, necessity.

ᛗ = E.    *Eh*, the horse.

ᚹ = W.    *Wynn*, joy.

ᚢ = U.    *Úr*, our.

ᛚ = L.    *Lagu*, water.

ᚠ = F.    *Feoh*, fee, or wealth.

"The 'Menologium,' or poetical Anglo-Saxon Calendar of the tenth century, says that St Helen's day of Cross is May 3; and then adds that six days afterwards comes 'sumor to tūne.'"
—SKEAT.

The passage runs thus :—

" With leafy trees and plants arrayed in splendour
    Fair, dainty May comes tripping to the town ;
The selfsame day when in supreme surrender,
    Philip and James their earthly lives laid down ;
        'Twas love to God on high
        Bade them thus bravely die.

Yet two days more, and by God's grace 'twas given
    To Helena the best of trees to find,
On which the great Creator, Lord of Heaven,
    Bore mortal anguish, so He loved mankind ;
        His Father, throned on high,
        Suffer'd Him thus to die.

And so, the first week after, but a day,
        Glad summer to the town
        Brings rays, that glancing down,
Shed genial warmth upon the chilly way."
          —Translated from ' Menologium,'
          Grein's edition, ll. 75-90.

·

# 'ELENE.'

N.B.—*The numbering of the lines is according to the original.*

## I.

SWIFT in the tale of time had fleeted
    Hundreds two and thirty-three
Winters for the world completed,
    Since heaven's Lord in low degree
In this mid-earth a man was born        5
To shed o'er faithful hearts a heavenly morn.

Six years the sceptre of the Roman
    Had held the leader Constantine ;[1]        10
His spear and shield against the foeman
    Guarded his folk with mood benign ;

[1] Constantine, a general in the Roman army, became Emperor in 306 A.D., seventy-nine years later than the date mentioned by the poet.

Great 'neath the skies his power grew,—
A prince of men, a righteous ruler true.


Through him God wrought with power wondrous,
  In mid-earth [1] many men to aid ;           15
Vengeance to wreak, and weapons thunderous
  Wield till the foemen fled afraid.
War waged the tribes ; with din earth trembled,
The Goths and Huns their heathen hosts assembled.    20


On came the Franks and Hugas streaming,
  Girt for the onset ; sword and spear
And twisted war-links sternly gleaming,
  With deafening shouts their flags they rear,    25
  And clash of shields as they draw near ;
Huge hosts together ; all behold them ;
Onward the nations march ; who can withhold them ?


War in the wood the wolf was crying,
  Hid not the secrets of the fray;
On the foes' track the eagle flying,    30
  With dewy feather sang his lay;
Quick from the cities all the warriors came,
The bravest whom the King of Huns for war might name.

---

[1] According to the Teutonic mythology, the earth occupies a place mid-way between heaven and hell.

Marched the huge host, its line enforcing                35
   With chosen legions, till it stood
Where, distant Danube's waters coursing,
   The spearmen rest beside the flood ;
There, where the squadrons stay before the slaughter,
They hear the host's loud hum, the rushing water.

Proud Rome to quell, to sack and plunder                40
   Was their design.   Soon as 'twas known
That foemen lurked the ramparts under,
   Came a swift message from the throne,
To summon out, against the foes assailing,            45
All who in warfare brave were and unfailing.

With warlike weapons soon the Roman,                  46
   Fight-famed, was ready for the fray ;
Rode round their leader, though the foeman
   In greater numbers rode than they ;              50
Clashed then the shield ; the war-clubs rattle,'
Onward the king rides with his host to battle.

O'erhead the dusky raven flying                       52
   With greedy croak pursued their course ;
Ran the horn-bearers, heralds crying,
   The charger pawed the ground ; the force         55
Quick at the signal's sound, assembled,
The monarch, horror-stricken, trembled.

With dismal fear and dire dismay,                57
   He saw the alien force
Of Huns and Goths who gathered lay
   About the water's course ;                60
A countless host.  His bosom heaved,
How e'er could victory be achieved,
Or such a monstrous force o'erthrown
By one so small and feeble as his own ?          65


But forward !   Ne'er from battle shrink !
He camped beside the river's brink,
So near the foe throughout the night,
Since he had seen them pass in sight.
He lay amid his host that night,
   And to his sense in dreaming             70
Appeared a vision of delight,
   Of fair and beauteous seeming ;
Noble, in manly form it came ;—
A knight of old heroic fame
Thus might have awed him in his seeming,
Such had he never seen, awake or dreaming.


He saw, and straight from slumber started,       75
   With boar-helm decked ; the shining guest
   Spake quickly, him by name addressed ;—
(And lo ! the veil of night was parted :—)

Thee, Constantine! so be it now revealed,
The Lord of Hosts, who fate alone can wield
The angels' King will covenant to shield. 80

"Let not the threats of foes distress thee,
    The alien hosts in battle-line;
Look up to heaven, the Lord will bless thee,
    Will send thee help, sure victory's sign." 85
Straight stood he ready at the heavenly hest,
He opened wide the treasure of his breast,
    Just as the dear peace-weaver bade,
    The herald who had made him glad.

Beyond the cloudy vault he looked, and shining
    He saw the Tree of Glory decked with gold; 90
Rare glittering jewels were the Rood enshrining,
    And on it, writ in light, he could behold
In letters clear the words: "Thou with this sign
Shalt overcome in shock of battle dire,
Drive back the foe, and make the victory thine." 

Back, as it came, then flashed the heavenly fire; 95
    The herald with it flew
Afar to join the sinless choir.
    More blithe the Emperor grew,—
Care in the leader's breast was quickly quelled,
When he that beauteous vision had beheld.

B

## II.

SCARCELY was lost to sight the symbol glorious,            99
    In highest skies revealed to Constantine,            100
When he, the warriors' ward, the chief victorious,
    Bounteous ring-giver, king of lordly line,
Commanded straight a standard-cross to fashion,
Like that, an emblem of the Saviour's passion.

Bade then at dawn, ere yet the sun shone o'er them,            105
    Waken the warriors, rouse the storm of swords;
Bear high the standard with the cross before them,
    Carry God's sign amid the hostile hordes,
Before the armies bid the trumpets blare
With clangour loud, as they for war prepare.

Rejoiced the raven at the battle coming,            110
    The dewy-feathered eagle saw them go;
Howled the wild wolf, in farthest forest roaming,
    Horror of bloodshed terrified the foe.
Forward they rushed, shields broke and arrows sped,
Flung lances till the field was strewn with dead.            115

Showers of arrows on the death-doomed dashing,
   Spears o'er the shield's bright rim their victims found,
And biting darts from fiery fingers flashing,                    120
   Daunted the foe, and dealt grim death around ;
On rushed the Romans, fearless on the field,
Splintered with swords fell many a glittering shield.

Then was the flag of victory high upholden,
   Sounded the song of triumph through the air,
Glittered the plain with spears and visors golden,              125
   While the fell foe sank down in dire despair,
And when the holy cross the Roman raised,                       130
Fast fled the Huns, affrighted and amazed.

And far and wide the alien force was scattered,
   Some on the war-path life had nearly left ;
Others the cities sought with senses shattered,
   Rescued from ruin in the rocky cleft,                   135
In forts that o'er the dashing Danube frown ;
While some the billowy waters swallowed down.

Joy filled the Roman ranks ; the heathens flying
   They followed on from dawn till evening fell ;         140
Death-dealing darts, weapons with vipers vying,
   Baffled the buckler-bearers all too well ;
Scarce of that Hunnish horde might one depart,
To seek his home, or cheer his broken heart.

Thus in the conflict victory obtaining,
   By God Almighty blessed was Constantine ;        145
Great 'neath the heavens, renown in mid-earth gaining,
   He triumphed through the high and holy sign ;
The warriors' guardian richly now might deck
His shield with jewels from the battle's wreck.        150

Then bearing high that buckler bright,
   By trusty thanes attended,
He sought for men who learning's height
   Had valiantly ascended,
Men who, in ancient lore their mind-thoughts steeping,        155
Wisdom for warriors treasured in their keeping.

He scanned his gleaming cohorts, and challenged them to
   tell
If old or young among them dwelt who could interpret        160
   well,
Who was the Lord of Glory, the "God who with this
   sign,
Himself to me revealing, has made the victory mine ;
And what this happy token, whence power flowed to me,
To beat the foemen backward, by that all-surpassing Tree."        165

All silent stood the swordsmen ; no answer could they
   find,
To say for what the emblem victorious was designed,

Though they who were the wisest, before the ranks made
    known,
That they without a doubt believed 'twas from Heaven's   170
    King alone.
Then those on whom through baptism had shone the light
    supreme,
Though few they were, grew light of heart, as in a blissful
    dream,


For now before the Emperor they might tell the Gospel   175
    story,
How He, the Lord of Spirits, throned in Trinity of glory,
Was born, the might of monarchs, and with many a pierc-
    ing pang,
The blessed Son of God upon the tree of pain did hang,   180
In presence of the people; such pity had he felt
For those who in the devil's bonds in hopeless misery
    dwelt.


How He on men had grace bestowed, e'en by that emblem
    high
Which to the Emperor had appeared, the sign of victory
Over the heathen hordes, and how, when laid within the
    tomb
Rose the third day, no longer held within that place of   185
    gloom,

The Glory of the heroes,—the Lord of human kind,—
And into heaven ascended. Thus with a prudent mind,

In ghostly mysteries to the king spake they who all had
    learned
Sylvester's lore.[1]   Thereat the heart of Constantine was   190
    turned;
Baptism he took, and from that hour his footsteps never
    strayed
From walking day by day with Him whose will he now
    obeyed.

[1] Sylvester I., Pope from 314 to 335 A.D.

## III.

NOW joyed the lordly treasure-giver,
    He who in combat courage showed ;
Within his spirit, like a river,
    A new and holy pleasure flowed ;
His hope grew high, his drooping heart was cheered,
By Him who reigns in highest heaven insphered.


And thus, that Ruler's spirit dwelling
    Within his heart both day and night,
Led him for ever to be telling
    The Ruler's law with deep delight ;
Thus the gold-friend of men, of warlike fame,
Took willing service in Jehovah's name.


So when the great spear-hurler, who the hosts to battle
    led,
Had found through learned scribes, with whom the books
    of God he read,

Where 'mid the clamour of the crowd, upon the tree of
    pain,
The Ruler of the skies had hung, through fraud and malice   205
    slain
(So the old arch-deceiver had misled the Jewish race,
To crucify the Lord Himself, the King of highest place,   210
And for that deed in misery to pass unending days
Condemned they were for ever) ; then the glorious Saviour's
    praise
So filled the mind of Constantine, the foremost of the folk,
That of that glorious tree alone he ever thought and spoke,
And bade his mother o'er the flood depart with chosen   215
    band
Of warriors brave, to seek with care in distant Jewish land
Where, hidden 'neath the holy soil, the tree of glory lay,
The cross of Him the noble King.   No moment of delay
Brooked Helena.   The welcome words she sought not to   220
    gainsay,
But ready soon for pilgrimage which to her heart seemed
    sweet,
She did the bidding of her son with ready, willing feet.
Then in hot haste the men prepare to cross the heaving   225
    flood,
Sea-chargers bound and ready along the margin stood ;
And lo ! the queen comes nobly, her legions with her
    come,
To tempt the bounding billows.   The pride of lordly Rome   230

There by the Mid-sea standeth, and o'er the blooming
    meads
Band after band is flocking, and loading the sea-steeds
With war-shirts, swords and bucklers; while many a warrior
    bold,
Full many men and women too the great sea-coursers   235
    hold,
And o'er the homes of monsters the foamy vessels glide,
Steep-sided ships, that with a rush o'er wavy waters ride;
Oft on the sounding gunwale smote a billow from the
    surges,
Sang the wild sea, as o'er its face the bounding fleet it
    urges.
Ne'er have I heard, before or since, that o'er the billows   240
    high
A woman led a force with power like that to charm the
    eye.
Who saw them o'er the whale's path go, might see the
    timbers racing,
Sea-coursers dancing under sail, the merry chargers   245
    chasing.
Blithe-hearted were the heroes all, with hopes and courage
    high;
The queen was fain to sail with such a gallant company.
And when the water-fastnesses the ringéd prows had
    passed,
And into port in Palestine had safely sailed at last,     250

They left their sea-beat ships to rock at anchor on the
    tide,
The wave-worn vessels there the fate of heroes to abide,
Till homeward wending with her hosts, again the warrior-
    queen
Might seek the old sea-dwellings.   Then soon on shore   255
    were seen
The splendid coat of mail, the woven corselet, blade of
    might,
The visor strong, and boar-topped casque, the foe with fear
    to smite.
Around their noble queen the cohorts gather with their
    lances,
Fit for the fray, in set array, each warlike wight advances.   260
High swells with joy each valiant heart, the Emperor to
    obey,
His legates bold, well-armed they hold through Palestine
    their way.
With glittering jewels set in gold, full many a man is
    dight,
The Emperor's gift.   And Helena dwells to her heart's
    delight,
With courage high and steady mind, on th' Emperor's   265
    command,
That she o'er many a battle-plain should seek the Jewish
    land,

With warriors tried, a chosen troop ; shield-bearers, cham-
    pions good ;—
And so not long they lingered, ere the countless multi-   270
    tude
Of famed lance-warriors with their queen in high Jerusalem   275
    stood.

---

## IV.

BADE Helena the citizens, the wisest far and near,
    Each man who words of wisdom knew, in council to
      appear,
Those who the hidden things of God most truly could    280
    impart,
Explain the heavenly mysteries with deep mind and faithful
    heart.
Flocked then from far in mighty host a company of those
Whom, Moses' holy law to teach, the Jewish people
    chose,
In number nigh three thousand ; and with words the noble
    queen
Thus to these Hebrew sages spake : "I verily have seen    285
Through mysteries in the book of God written by holy
    seers,
That to the King of Glory ye were precious in past years,    290
Doughty and to Jehovah dear.    But ah ! in froward
    mood,
From wisdom's ways ye wandered, and in folly's pathway
    stood.

Him ye rejected, Him ye doomed, who came to bring release
By glorious power from fetters fast and flames that never
    cease.
Foully ye spat upon His face who gave your eyes their light,   295
Sight after blindness gave anew, and from the baleful might
Of hellish spirits saved.  And Him ye doomed to cruel
    death,
Who many of the human race awoke to life and breath,   300
Giving for death that life primeval made at first for man ;   305
And so ye, blind of spirit, truth with lies to mix began,
Hatred with mercy, and in cruel baseness wrong devised ;
Henceforth in deep damnation dwell, ye who have God
    despised.
His glorious majesty ye judged, and lived in errors vain,   310
And thoughts of darkness to this day.  Go quickly back
    again,
And seek out men of power, within whose souls are richly
    dwelling
The holy word and righteous laws, who all your race ex-   315
    celling,
Can truly tell and give to me answer before your face,
To each and all the signs whereof I ask them in this
    place."
Silent and sad of mood each one, the law-learned men
    depart,
With fear alarmed, by care o'ercome, to seek with anxious   320
    heart

For men whose souls most deeply were by sacred writ
    inspired,
That they might to the queen return the answer she
    desired,
Nor good nor ill withhold; then through the concourse  325
    searching wide,
A thousand earnest men they found, who deeply had
    descried
The story of the Jews of old, and had in soul grown great.
Thronged these in troops around the throne, where high in
    royal state
· The warlike queen magnificent, in golden raiment, sate.  330
Before the men then Helena thus spake: "O heroes
    wise,
Hear now the word and wisdom of the sacred mysteries!
Lo! ye have heard old prophets tell, how He from whom  335
    life sprang
In child's estate was born, the Lord of might.  As Moses
    sang,
Israel's great guardian, saying thus : 'To you is born a
    Child
In secret, great of might, whose maiden mother, meek and
    mild,
Knew not the love of man.'  Of Him King David, wisest  340
    lord,
The sire of Solomon, the prince of warriors, spake this
    word :

'God, the beginning of all things, the Lord in battle   345
    glorious,
On my right hand, before my eyes, the Lord of Hosts
    victorious,
Glorious in countenance I saw, the Lord of Life and
    Glory,
And from the sight I ne'er away have turned throughout
    life's story.'
So too Isaiah, prophet deep, by breath of God inspired,   350
Among you to the many spake, in words with wisdom fired :
'A tender branch have I raised up, a Child to me is given,
Whom I with happiness have blest, and holy peace from
    heaven ;
And yet they scorned and hated me, no righteous thought   355
    had they,
Nor wisdom,—e'en the weary beasts they drive and smite
    each day,
Know their preserver, practise no revenge for suffered ill,   360
Nor hate the friends who give them food. But wayward
    Israel
Hath ne'er considered me, nor known, my people void of
    thought,
Though I throughout the ages past great things for them
    have wrought.'

## V.

" LO! we through holy books have heard of stainless
        glory gained
For you, and wealth of might, by that great God who Moses
    trained
To teach how ye the King of Heaven in all things should    365
    obey ;
Yet, wearied soon of that, His glorious law ye did gainsay,
Despised the Lord of Lords, Him who had heaven and
    earth created,
Forsook His law, and all your powers to error dedicated.    370
Go quickly now, and find again those who in ancient writ
Most deeply versed, by wisdom's power can best interpret it,
Your law—and give to me through knowledge wide an
    ˙answer fit."
Then went the mighty host of heroes, haughty, sad at    375
    heart,
Five hundred of the wisest men they quickly set apart
From all the other people, those in knowledge deeply    380
    learned,
Who in their spirit wisdom high most clearly had discerned ;

These guardians of the city, men of wisdom one and all,
After a little space the queen then summoned to the hall.
She looked upon the men, and thus in flowing language    385
    spake:
"Oh why, by folly led, do ye God's holy laws forsake?
Why do ye wicked deeds so oft, ye men of misery,
And from the teaching of your sires each day yet farther
    fly?
Blindly repentance ye disdained, and far and wide ignored    390
That the Child born in Bethlehem was the Son of Heaven's
    Lord,
The first among the princes,—and this though the law ye
    knew,
The prophets' word, yet sinfully ye still denied the true."    395
Then in one breath they answered: "So we knew from days
    of old
The Hebrews' law, which at God's ark was to our fathers
    told ;
But this we cannot understand, why thus in anger stern,    400
O lady, thou accusest us. What crime, we fain would
    learn,
Have we committed in this place, 'gainst thee what wrong
    have done?"
Spake Helena before the men, concealment made she    405
    none,—
Loud to the hosts the woman cried: "Haste, and be quickly
    gone,

C

And single out from all your ranks those who with wisdom
    blest,
Of greatest strength in soul and mind among you are
    possest,
That boldly and unfalteringly they may declare to me
All that I seek from them to know, in faith and verity."    410
Forth went they from the council, as bade the mighty queen,
She who the cities boldly swayed,—and sad in heart and
    mien,
With earnest thought and prudent mind, to name the deed
    they sought,
Which they amid the people 'gainst the Emperor had    415
    wrought,
Thus earning blame from Helena.    Then spake before the
    throng
One Judas, who was wise of speech, and in the Scripture
    strong :
"Well know I what she seeks : it is the Tree of victory,
On which the Prince of nations hung, as man from error    420
    free,
Yea, God's own Son unsinning, whom our fathers hated
    sore,
So that they hanged Him on a lofty tree in days of yore.

That was a deed of horror.    And the time    425
Has come, when we our minds with courage guiding,
    Must watch lest we betray that deadly crime,

And where the holy Tree in secret hiding
　　After the struggle fierce to rest was laid,　　　　430
Lest all the wise old Scriptures be o'erthrown,
The patriarchs' lore no longer hold its own.

No longer then might Israel's race in glory
　　Teach men her laws, and earth's dominions quell ;—
This secret known, she falls, as once the story　　435
　　Zaccheus, my brave grandsire, used to tell
In ancient wisdom to my father bold,
Who, ere he left the world, his offspring told,—

And thus he spake : ' If in thy life-days here,　　440
　　Questions of wise men, strife amid the sages
About the glorious Tree, should greet thine ear,
　　On which was hung the King of all the ages,　　445
Heaven's Ruler, Lord of truth, the Son of peace,
Then say, ere yet thy pulse to beat shall cease :

　　" Should this be known, the fatal hour
　　　　Comes for the Jewish race,
　　When crafty foes, with hostile power
　　　　Shall hold a ruler's place.　　　　450
But ever shall *their* glory, greater growing,
　*Their* power with rolling ages stronger be,
World without end with joys eternal glowing,
　　Who praise the Crucified eternally." '

## VI.

" THEN boldly to my sire I answer made,
            E'en to the law-learned one, the ancient sage :     455
'How could, within the region of this world,
Such thing e'er be, that on the Holy One
Our fathers impiously, to end His life,
Could lay their hands (so thwarted was their wit)
If they had known before, He was the Christ,                   460
Lord of the Heavens, the Maker's very Son,
The Spirit's Saviour?'    Answer then my sire,
My father, wise in mind, thus gave in words :
'Knowest thou not, O youth, God's mighty power,
The Saviour's name?    It is unutterable                       465
By man below, nor can on earth-way any
Search out the Lord.    Never this nation's counsels
I sought to know, but from their sins I stood
Apart, lest shame my soul should overtake.                     470
Yea, oft I earnestly their wrong withstood,
When subtle scribes I saw in council sitting,
Seeking how they the great Creator's Son
Might crucify, Guardian and Lord of all,                       475

Angels and men, the noblest of earth's sons.
And yet they could not do Him thus to death,
Unhappy men, as erewhile they had deemed,
Nor quite by sorrow slay, though He some time
His ghost upon the grievous tree gave up,                480
Victorious Son of God.   After a space,
Creation's Lord from cruel cross was taken,
Glory of Glories, and within the tomb
Tarried three nights, to darkest dungeon doomed ;—       485
And the third day, living, the Light of Light
Again arose, and to His thanes appeared,
True Lord of Victory, Himself revealed
In glory great.   Then after many days
Thy brother bold the bath of baptism took,               490
Holding the faith.   And for his love of the Lord,
Stephen was stoned with stones, yet rendered not
Wrong for that wrong, but for his fiercest foes,
In patience praying to the Lord of Glory,
Begged Him no vengeance on that crime to wreak,          495
That they, by Saul incited, had of life
Bereft the Blessed One, from malice free,
As Saul so many of Christ's faithful folk,
In wicked hate, to pain and death had doomed.            500
Yet God had mercy on him afterward,
And when Creation's God, mankind's Redeemer,
Had changed his name, no longer Saul to be,              505
But holy Paul the preacher, he the source

Of blessing grew to many sorrowing souls.
And than Saint Paul no better was there found
'Mid teachers of the Gospel, 'neath the sky,
'Mid all of women born within the world,
Yea, though he bade them Stephen slay with stones,
Thy blessed brother, on yon mountain height.     510
   " ' Now shalt thou hear, O hero mine beloved,
How full of mercy is the mighty Ruler,
Though oft we crimes commit 'gainst His command,
If we the wounds of sin again would heal,
Repenting of our wrong, to Him return,           515
And cease from sinful ways for evermore.
Thenceforth in truth, I and my father dear,
No longer doubted that the Lord of Life,
God of all Glory, leader of the living,          520
A loathly torment suffered for the need
Most woful of the wretched race of man.
Now bid I thee by secret lore to learn,
O dearest son, that never words of scorn,
Of spite or evil-speaking, thou may'st utter,
Or cruel contradiction 'gainst God's Son.        525
So shalt thou earn eternal life in heaven,
That boon most blessed shall be given to thee.'
'Twas thus my father, in the far-off days,
Me, young, unwitting, warned with wisdom's words,
Taught with true teaching (Simon was his name ;  530
A man of seasoned speech).   Now ye have learned

What to your musing mind most fit may seem
To tell this queen, if of the Tree she ask you,
Now ye the spirit of my mind-thought know."        535
     Answered him then the wisest 'mid the troop,
Speaking with words : "We never until now
Heard any hero 'mid this folk but thee,
Or other thane, such wondrous words make known    540
Of hidden mysteries.   Do what seems good,
O wise in ancient lore, if thou be asked
Amid the troop of men.   He prudence needs
And weighty words, and wisdom of the wise,
Who to the noble queen shall answer give           545
Before the mighty host assembled here."

## VII.

A WAR of words then waged the men, sought out on
    either side,
Hither and thither weighed and thought, each way the
    question tried;
Then come the learned troop to where the folk assembled
    stand,
High rise the heralds' voices: "Hear the Emperor's com-    550
    mand:
O heroes, to the lofty hall ye by this queen are bidden,
That of your council's wise decrees may nought from her
    be hidden.
Then rightly to report, where stand the people all assembled,
With wisest prudence be prepared, O men, be naught dis-
    sembled."
With solemn mien, soon ready to obey the hard behest,
The guardians of the people marched, by mighty power    555
    possessed,
Wisdom to utter.  Asked the queen, the heroes full of
    woe,
About the ancient writings and the prophets, long ago,    560

Wise men of holy thought, who in the world had sung ere-
    while
Of God's own Child, and where the Prince had suffered
    torments vile,
True Son of the Creator, so the souls of men He loved.
Harder than stone they stood, and stern, by naught to    565
    answer moved;
Ne'er to their grievous foe would they the hidden truth
    make known,
But with firm front her questions foiled and baffled, one by
    one;
Said that through life they ne'er before aught like to this    570
    had heard:
Then haughtily spake Helena, her breast with anger stirred:
" Truth will I speak, a truth that shall for ever fixed remain;
If ye who stand before me still make all my pleading vain    575
With your deceitful dealing, then shall fire your dwelling
    shatter,
And seething, sword-like flames your bones to all the winds
    shall scatter.
In flickering flames ye then shall feel that this one lie could    580
    sever
You, soul and body, from your place within the world for
    ever.
In vain your words ye strive to prove, ye who in sin abiding,
Beneath the veil of vile deceit the truth have long been
    hiding.

Such secret powers and dire events why seek ye to
    conceal?"
Then, seized with dread of death that should their doom
    with horror seal,
One they gave up, who, well endowed, his words with   585
    wisdom wielded,
Among his kinsmen Judas hight—him to the queen they
    yielded :
Said, "He is wise o'er others, he will tell the truth when
    bidden,
Answer thy asking, and unveil events that fate has
    hidden ;—
Faithful from first to last.  No man can boast of kindred   590
    higher,
Wise is he in the war of words ; a prophet was his sire.
Bold is he in the throng of men ; and from his boyhood's
    day,
Answers adroit to all he gave, such power within him lay.
Him in the multitude of men, deep wisdom shall inspire   595
Things hidden to reveal, according to thy heart's desire."
In peace then bade she each man seek his home, and one
    alone,
Judas, as hostage held, and begged the truth he would
    make known,
About the cross that in dark cell so long had hidden been,   600
And so she bade him step aside, with solemn earnest
    mien.

Then to the solitary man spake Helena the queen :
"Two things I offer thee this day, which thou may'st
    choose between.
Say, wilt thou life or death?   Be ready now at once to say   605
Which of the two thou wilt elect to be thy lot this day."
Judas to her made answer (gnawing grief his soul devoured,
The sovereign's anger, for the queen his spirit overpowered):   610
" How shall the wanderer in the desert waste,
In want and weariness who treads the moor,
O'ercome by hunger, when before his eyes
A loaf and stone together he beholds,
The hard and soft, how can he with the stone   615
Vanquish his gnawing hunger, leave the loaf,
And, wooing want, the needed food forsake,
Despise the better, having both at hand?"

## VIII.

THEN openly before the folk Helena answer gave:
    "Wilt thou in heaven with angels dwell, on earth a   620
    blessing have,
A victor's triumph in the sky? then quickly, truly
    say,
Where lies the holy tree of God, under what spot of   625
    clay,
That ye so long, with deadly wrong, from men have hid
    away?"
Spake Judas (grief was in his mind, his heart by fire con-
    sumed,
Woe was his portion, whether he to forfeit heaven were
    doomed,
With all its joy, and also of the present suffer loss,
This realm beneath the skies, or whether he should show   630
    the cross):
"How can I find what many years have hidden as they
    rolled?
Over two hundred winters now the mystery enfold;

I cannot tell their number; there have lived on earth
    since then,

Men who have gone before us, wise and good and prudent   635
    men.

And I in later times was born a boy; I nothing know,    640

Nor can I keep in mind what passed so very long ago."

Him answered Helena: "And how, amid such men of
    might,

Have ye remembered all the deeds the Trojans wrought in
    fight?

More ancient was the terror of that famous war of old,    645

Than of this dread event, brought nearer as the ages
    rolled.

Well do ye know their number, who on gory battle-field,

Losing their lances, drooped and died beneath the shelter-   650
    ing shield,

And ye have marked their sepulchres upon each rocky
    height,

What time and in what place they fell, ye have not failed
    to write."

Spake Judas, sorrow-smitten: "Great the need, O lady
    mine,

That we that stormy struggle set in writing line by line,   . 655

That fury of the nations; but ne'er yet by man pro-
    claimed

Have we that other wonder heard, which thou to us hast
    named."

Answered him then the noble queen : " Too much thou 660
　　now deniest,
And falsely of the tree of life thou now to me repliest,
When thou a little while ago wert to thy people telling
The story of that wondrous Tree, in glory all excelling.' 665
Replied then Judas, that he half in sorrow had been
　　speaking,
And half in doubt and fear lest fate were vengeance on
　　him wreaking :
To him the Emperor's mother : " Lo, we read in sacred 670
　　story,
That on Mount Calvary hung the Son of God, the King of
　　Glory,
God's spiritual Son.　Now shalt thou nothing from me
　　hide
That in the Scripture stands, but show where, in this re-
　　gion wide,
Is Calvary, ere torments dire thy soul and body sever, 675
Doom for thy sins, that by the will of Christ I may for
　　ever
Cleanse all that place to be a help to all of human
　　race,
That God, the inmost thought of life, the Lord of power
　　and grace,
The God who to His armies glory gives in danger dire,
Helper of spirits, may my will with heavenly power 680
　　inspire."

Still stout of heart spake Judas : "Of the place I nothing
    know,
Nor know I where it lies, or aught belonging thereunto."
In angry mood then Helena : "By God's own Son I swear,
The God by mortals crucified, that thou shalt hunger bear,    685
Till thou in pain shalt yield the ghost before thy kins-
    men's eyes,
Unless at once thou turn to words of truth, and leave
    these lies."
Bade then at once the thralls to lead the living man away,    690
And thrust into a dried-up well (no tardy thralls were they),
Where he seven nights in misery, all joyless must remain,
In dungeon dark, by hunger held, and clasped by cruel
    chain,
Till the seventh day he cried aloud, by woful want laid    695
    low,
"I do adjure you, by the God of Heaven, to let me go
From out this den of torture, gnawing hunger's hated prey,
That I the holy cross may show, the truth reveal this day.    700
So hard the hunger, and so strong the chains that clasp me
    here,
So dire the torment, and so sore the suffering I must bear,
I can no more endure it, can the truth no more withhold,    705
About the tree of life, though folly so my heart did fold,
That all the truth ye fain would hear, too long remains
    untold."

## IX.

H IS earnest words heard Helena, his noble mien beheld,
  And she who there held sovereign sway, and all the
    heroes quelled,
Bade then undo the prison-doors, and ope the narrow cell,     710
That he no more in den of doom and dungeon dark might
    dwell.
Quickly her bidding they obeyed, and at the queen's com-
    mand,
From out the dungeon drew him, that he in their midst
    might stand;
Then up the mount together marched, stalwart and strong   715
    of mood,
Till where the King of Heaven, their Lord, was crucified,
    they stood,
The Son of God, upon the tree; still Judas could not say
(So weak he was through hunger) in what place in hiding
    lay
The holy cross, that crafty foes beneath the ground con-    720
    cealing,
Long in its lair had left to rest, no one its grave revealing.

Anon, as weak as water, spake the man in Hebrew thus :

"Saviour and Lord, man's Ruler, who by power glorious    725

Heaven and the earth hast made, and all the wide tumul-
tuous sea,

The boundless ocean vast, and all things everywhere that be,

And with Thy hands hast meted out the vast revolving
sky,

And who Thyself, of victory Lord, in state art throned on    730
high,

Above the noblest angel race, who flit in light through air,

And none of mortal kind may earth-ways leave and upward    735
fare

In human form amid that host of glorious heralds bright,

Whom Thou hast holy, heavenly made, Thy service their    740
delight.

There in eternal joy are six, in highest rank that shine,

And each is folded round about with glorious wings
divine.

Four of them, flying ceaselessly, watch o'er the service high

Of the great Judge eternal, who beholds them constantly.

And evermore, with voices clear, they praise in sweetest    745
hymn

The King of Heaven, and these the words (their name is    750
Cherubim) :

'Holy is the archangels' Lord, Prince of the Hosts on
high,

The earth is of His glory full, His power shows the sky.'

Two are there in that lofty place who dwell, of race vic-
    torious,

Their name is Seraphim, and they with flaming falchion   755
    glorious

Must o'er bright Paradise and life's fair tree keep holy
    guard;

The sharp blade trembles, and the rich-wrought steel with
    edges hard

Within their grasp shifts ever form and hue with horrid
    force.

Thus Thou, good Lord, of ever-varying life dost guide the   760
    course,

And from the skies didst headlong hurl Thy foes, the
    fiends of sin;

They fell to dwellings dark, doom and destruction found
    therein.

There, wreathed in flames, they writhe in pain within the
    dragon's claws.

In deepest misery sunk is he who would not keep Thy   765
    laws;

So full of vileness, exiled he, a bondsman must remain,

And since he sinned the first, must ever drag his cruel
    chain;

No more within that place of woe, dispute Thy word may he;   770

O God, the King of angels, if Thou wilt that Ruler be,

He who upon the cross did hang, and who in child's
    degree

Of Mary in this earth was born, though King of angels
    bright,

(And who, if not Thy sinless Son, ne'er had such works of   775
    might

In truth performed within the world, through all His earthly
    days,

Nor hadst Thou willed, O Lord of Hosts, Him from the   780
    dead to raise

Before the people, were He not Thy Son, as Thou hast
    said ;)

Father of Heaven, let then Thy sign before us all appear,

And hear us, as of old Thou Moses in his prayer didst   785
    hear,

When in that glorious day, O God, beneath the mountain-
    head,

The bones of Joseph Thou to him didst show. And thus
    I pray

That by that glorious sign, if so it be Thy will this day,

The great and priceless treasure, ages long from men con-   790
    cealed,

O Maker of the souls of men, be now to me revealed.

Father of Life, bid from that place a gladdening smoke
    arise,

Hovering in air beneath the spacious circuit of the skies.

More shall I thus believe Thee, and more gratefully   795
    confide

Without a doubt in Him who is the Christ, the Crucified,

That He is Saviour of the souls of men in very truth,
Almighty and Eternal King, who in unfading youth,
Ruling in yonder heavens that are for aye His glory telling,       800
World without end, has fixed on high His everlasting
    dwelling."

## X.

BEHOLD then from the spot a cloud ascending,
   Like smoke beneath the skies; the wondrous sight
Joy to the law-learned hero's heart is lending,      805
   With outstretched hands he hails it with delight.


He spake aloud: "Now I, the truth confessing,
   Know that Thou art the Saviour verily
Of all the world.  Be everlasting blessing      810
   And thanks, O glorious God of Hosts, to Thee;


"That Thou to me, the weary and the erring,
   Thy wondrous mysteries dost thus unfold.
O Son of God, men's best desires conferring,
   Who kingly glory at Thy birth didst hold,      815


"I pray that Thou the faults, than which none greater,
   Which I against Thy holiness have done,
No longer may'st remember, O Creator,
   But let me of that glorious host be one,

"Who live in light within that shining city,                820
    Where dwells my brother Stephen in renown,
Because he held with Thee, nor asked for pity,
    E'en 'neath the cruel stones that struck him down.


"His is the martyr's meed, unending glory,                825
    The wonders that he wrought are clearly written
In books, where all may read the famous story."
    Then fell he straight, with eager gladness smitten,


To digging 'neath the turf, till far below                830
    Full twenty feet, he found in space of gloom,
Down in a steep abyss there lurking low,
    Three cross-staves hidden in a narrow room,


Heaped o'er with earth, as them the God-forsaken,        835
    In days long vanished, had with earth o'erlaid,
The Jews, who 'gainst God's Son would hate awaken;
    They strayed in sin, nor righteous laws obeyed.


Then was his mind with joy uplifted greatly,             840
    Strong grew his spirit through the holy tree,
Inspired his heart, when he the beacon stately
    In its dark dwelling 'neath the earth could see.
Firm in his hands he seized the beacon holy,
And with the people raised it from its earth-grave lowly.

Strangers and princes now the city enter;                845
    Straightway the men, with bold and dauntless mien,
Plant the three crosses upright in their centre,
    In face of Helena the kneeling queen.


She, glad at heart, the hero's work beholding,           850
    Would have him say which was it of the three
On which the Son of God did hang, unfolding
    New hope for man in dire extremity.


" Lo, we to books of sacred writ have hearkened,
    That told us, by His side there suffered twain,      855
And He the third.   The light in heaven was darkened
    On that dread day.   Oh ! couldst thou but make plain,
On which of these three roods His life did yield
The Prince of angels, glory's guard and shield."


But Judas, knowing not the symbol glorious,              860
    Could give the queen no certain answer yet,
On which had hung the Son of God victorious,
    The Saviour, till he bade his followers set


The trees, with tumult, in the city great,              865
There, in its midst, the wonder to await,
By which the King Almighty from His throne
The holy cross should to the hosts make known.

Sat then the famed in fight, together singing ;
    Round the three roods the redesmen pondered well,
Till the ninth hour, when a new joy upspringing
    They found, and marvelled. Numbers none could    870
        tell
Of people thronged, and on a bier were bringing


A youth from whom the soul had newly fled.          875
    Came then great gladness Judas' heart to cheer ;
'Twas the ninth hour. A brave troop bore the
        bier ;
    He bade them on the ground to place the dead,


The lifeless one, the frame of breath bereft.
    Then deep in thought, as who the truth unfoldeth,
Over the house of life that life hath left,
    With outstretched hands two of the roods he
        holdeth.


Dead on the bier see yet the body lie ;             880
    Cold are the limbs, by mortal pangs o'erlaid.
Then the third holy cross is held on high ;
    It was but for this sign the dead had stay'd,
Till, o'er his head upreared, the Rood divine        885
Of heaven's Monarch should all-conquering shine.

Straight he arose, with soul anew endowed ;
  Body and spirit now have met again ;      890
Sang then the people praises long and loud,
  Praising with words the Father of all men
        And the true Son
        Of the Highest One,
To whom from creatures all be thanks and glory
Through endless ages' never-ending story.

## XI.

THEN deeply in the people's thought, by wonder strongly   895
        smitten,
The glorious wonders, as they ought to be, anew were
        written,
Which the great Lord of Hosts had wrought, leader to life
        unending,
Safety to find for human kind.   Behold the foe ascending,
The lying fiend, on wings through air.   Spake then the
        prince of hell,
Monster of horrid mien, who every ill remembered well :   900
"What man is this, who ancient strife renews, my slaves
        destroying,
Feeds former feuds, and plunders all my wealth for his en-
        joying ?
This is a ceaseless warfare.   Scarce had sinful souls   905
        begun
To dwell within my power, when hither comes this hated
        one,                          .
Whom firmly bound by chains of sin I until now believed,
And me of every right and all my riches has bereaved.   910

Such action is unjust.   The Saviour wrought me many
     woes
And crushing wrongs, He who in Nazareth to manhood
     rose.
No sooner was His childhood o'er, than He must master     915
     be
Of all I once called mine.   No claim to aught remains
     for me.
Broad is His realm on earth, while 'neath the skies my
     power is failing ;
Not even with laughter dare I mock the cross ; for bitter     920
     wailing
Is now again my lot, shut up within this narrow prison
By Him you call the Saviour.   Once through Judas hope
     had risen ;
Another Judas fails me now, and I, a castaway,
Fall, friendless, of all good bereft.   Could I but find the     925
     way
By wicked plots from out this land of exile to return !

     " Against thee I another will awaken,
         A king who thee with torments shall pursue,
     Thy doctrines all shall be by him forsaken,
         My ends unrighteous he shall gladly do ;

     " Thee shall he send into the worst and blackest     930
         Terror of woe, where tortures manifold

Shall visit thee, until thou courage lackest
  To own the King whom yonder cross did hold,

"Whom thou didst once obey." Then thus addressed him
  Judas, the wise in mind, in battle brave          935
(The Holy Ghost dwelt aye in him, and blessed him
  With glowing love, wisdom that like a wave

Flowed from the warrior's wit); thus wisely speaking:
  "Seek not," he said, "oh thou of evil lord,
Pain to renew, thus vilely vengeance wreaking          940
  On the great King, who to the abyss abhorred '

"Hath thrust thee down to torments for thy sinning,
  Who oft the dead made living by His word.          945
Know well, by folly thou, in the beginning,
  Forsook'st the light and joy of love's great Lord,

"And hence, with hellish flames around thee shooting,
  Hater of God, shalt bear an endless woe,          950
A doom eternal." Thus the loud disputing
  Heard Helena, of friend and bitter foe,

Noble and base; the sinful and the holy,          955
  Heard with deep joy the hellish fiend refuted,
Parent of sin,—and wondered how so wholly
  Wisdom and faith thus in brief space were rooted

In heart of simple man.   The King all-glorious         960
  She praised for double gift, both for the sight
Of that great tree, and of the faith victorious
  That in the hero's breast shone true and bright.         965

## XII.

THEN was told to all the people, 'mid the warriors
 was spread wide
That glorious morning tale, though some who God's com-
 mands would hide
Heard it with sorrow ; it was noised abroad where'er the   970
 strand
The sea embraces, in each camp and city of the land,—
That Christ's dear Rood, buried of old in earth, had now
 been found,
Most blest of signs e'er raised aloft 'neath Heaven's circuit   975
 round.
And to the Jews, unhappy men, 'twas a woful weird to
 dree,
Saddest of sorrows, from which naught on earth could set
 them free,
But to the Christians joy.   Then bade the queen send   980
 forth in haste
Heralds from all the warrior-host o'er ocean's billowy
 waste,

To Rome's great lord himself the wished-for tidings near to
    bring,

That the great sign of victory, by the grace of Heaven's   985
    King,

Was found where it in earth for ages long had hidden
    lain,

A sorrow to the saints, the Christian folk.  The king was
    fain,

Gleeful at heart, to hear the word that all his soul rejoiced,

Nor was there lack of men in gilded raiment, eager-voiced,   990

To ask the news from far.  What joy to him could
    greater be

In all the world, than the glad heart, that leapt exultingly

At the long-wished-for tale which o'er the eastern ways had   995
    brought

These heralds, lords of war, how they far Palestine had
    sought,

And safely o'er the swan's path with their queen had
    thither fared.

There to return the emperor bade them quickly be prepared.

Soon as they heard his answer, no longer might they stay,   1000

Hail to victorious Helena he bade them bring, if they

Safe o'er the billowy seas might pass, and happily attain,

Stout-hearted heroes, to the holy city once again.   1005

Bade Constantine the heralds then give Helena command

That she should build a church, there on the mountain-
    height to stand,

On Calvary, a temple of the Lord, for Christ a shrine,        1010
For their souls' weal and help to men, where once the
    Rood divine
Was found, most glorious of trees e'er seen by mortal  1015
    eyne.
This she performed, when loving friends had brought her
    from the west
Their message o'er the sea.   Those who in arts were skilled
    the best
She bade seek out, and chiefly those for work in stone  1020
    most famed,
To raise upon that place a house, God's temple to be
    named.
Thus was her soul inspired from heaven ; she bade them
    deck with gold
And gems the holy Tree, with jewels brightest to behold ;  1025
With highest art to deck, and then within a silver shrine
Lock fast.   And there the Tree of life, vict'ry's most
    blessed sign,
Dwelt evermore unperishing.   And evermore dwells there
Help for the sick in every woe, in conflict and in care.    1030
There through that holy thing, the grace of help from
    heaven descending
Uplifts their soul ; thus Judas, at the appointed season's
    ending,
In bath baptismal cleansed, and to his life's dear guardian
    true,

Confessed the Christ.   Then strong the faith within his   1035
      bosom grew,
Since in his heart the Spirit of all comfort took His dwelling,
Inspiring him to holiness.   The better part excelling,
The joy of heaven he chose, the worse he cast aside, refusing
Idolatry, false doctrine, and the law of sin, and choosing   1040
The King Eternal, the Creator Infinite,
Merciful God, and Ruler of all power and might.

E

## XIII.

THUS was baptised he who with strong endeavour
    Full many a time ere now had sought the light ;    1045
Within his breast a longing urged him ever
    On to the better life, to glory bright.

        Was it not fate's decree
        He thus should faithful be
        To God within this earthly sphere,
        And reverent to his Saviour dear?    1050

Then to the folk straightway it was proclaimed,
    When Helena had called to council grave
Eusebius, bishop of Rome (most famed
    For wisdom in the meetings of the brave),

That he might Judas in Jerusalem place,    1055
    A bishop in that holy town to be,
God's chosen temple through the Spirit's grace,
    By knowledge ;—and by wisdom's new decree

Gave him the name of Cyriacus, henceforth
  Within the city's gates to be his name,—
Vow'd henceforth to his Lord,—a name of worth.        1060
  Still on the new-told tale of glorious fame

Mused Helena, and greatly had in thought
  The nails that pierced the Saviour's hands and feet,        1065
Which the blest body to the cross had caught
  Of Heaven's mighty Lord.   Then 'gan entreat

Cyriacus the Christian's queen, that still
  Once more by glorious gifts and Spirit's might        1070
About those wondrous things he would fulfil
  Her bidding, and reveal them soon to sight.

Then to the bishop Helena the word
  Spake boldly: "Thou, oh shield of men, hast done
Rightly, hast shown the rood on which the Lord        1075
  Of heaven, mankind's helper, God's own Son,

"Hung, by the hands of heathen men fast bound,
  Saviour of men.   Still in my secret mind
The wish devours me, that beneath the ground
  Those precious hidden things thou yet might'st find ;—        1080

"So deeply buried, so in darkness lost
  Are they.   Ah me! my heart despairing droops,

Sadly complains, by waves of sorrow tost,
    Until the Leader high of angel troops,

"Th' Almighty Father, holy from the height,    1085
    Saviour of men, to me this blessing send,
To find the nails.   Amid those beings bright,
    Best messenger, oh! let thy pray'rs ascend

"E'en now, and humbly beg the warriors' Strength,    1090
    Glory's great King, that He to thee reveal
That treasure lying hid in earth, at length,
    Which dark recesses still from men conceal."

Then he with heart inspired, the bishop holy,    1095
    Began the people's mind to cheer and raise,
And with a band of men, in worship lowly,
    Gladly went Cyriacus, with fervent praise,

His face o'er Calvary bent, nor strove to hide
    His heart's desire, and in the Spirit's power    1100
With meekness to the Lord of angels cried,
    That He would aid him in this trying hour,—

Unveil the hidden, and confirm his thought
    Of where within that field the nails might rest.
Then as they looked, a wonder straight was wrought
    By the great Father and the Spirit blest,—    1105

In form of fire from out the earth it came,
  Where, hidden by men's craft and subtlety,
Deep buried lay the nails.   A rushing flame
  Sudden, with more than sunlight filled the sky.      1110

The wonder-worker thus their wish had granted;
  The people saw, like stars in heaven that glow,
Or gold and gems in earthly soil new planted,
  The nails from out their hiding-place below

Gleam brightly.   Then the joyous crowd exulted,      1115
  For wish fulfilled to God they glory gave;
Now one in heart are they who once insulted
  And turned from Christ, misled by error grave.      1120

Yea, we ourselves, they said, have seen the token
  Of victory, God's miracle most true;
Of which erewhile we slightingly have spoken
  With lying words.   But now upon our view

New light hath dawned, and truly told the story
  Of what has passed.   For this in highest height
To the great God who reigns in heaven be glory;—      1125
  Then glowed the heart anew with fresh delight

Of him, the people's bishop, who, believing
  The Son of God, was led to life more holy;

With awe-struck mien the blessed nails receiving,
  He gave them to the queen with reverence lowly.          1130

Thus, as the noble queen before had bidden,
  Cyriacus all her sovereign will had done;
Weeping was heard, the tears welled forth unchidden,
  Flowed down the cheek, though sorrow there was none.

Glad tears fell o'er the gold threads intertwining,          1135
  Granted now wholly was the queen's request,
And in unclouded faith her knee inclining,
  She worshipped there, in bliss supremely blest,

The gift that soothed her grief; and with thanksgiving
  She cried to God, the Lord of Victory,          1140
That what since time began had cheered the living
  Often by words, she now might clearly see.

With wisdom's heavenly gift her soul abounded,
  And in her noble breast came to abide          1145
The Holy Ghost, while all her ways surrounded
  God's Son victorious, as her guard and guide.

## XIV.

THEN in her inmost soul the queen, in sacred mysteries
  learned,
With holy zeal from heaven inspired, for heavenly glory
  yearned.
For was it not the God of Hosts, the Father throned in   1150
  heaven,
Who to her strivings on the earth such blessed end had
  given ?
And had not ancient sages sung of old from first to last,
In all its order due, the wondrous thing that now had   1155
  passed ?
Thus now began the people's queen, inspired by heavenly
  grace,
With holy zeal and earnest care to seek in what high place
And splendid way, the sacred nails might to all eyes be
  shown,
To gladden human hearts, yet by the will of God alone.   1160
Anon she bade to council call a sage of prudent mind,
Who, versed in runes, could render rede, by craft the truth
  could find,

And  promised  straight,  if  he  to  wisest  deed  would  point  1165
   the way,

She by his counsel meekly would abide, nor aught gainsay.

Bold speech he gave : " 'Tis fitting now, oh noble queen, for  1170
   thee,

Within thy thought to hold God's word, the sacred mystery,

And do the king's behest, since happily thy soul and
   earnest mind

Victory have gained, through grace of God, the Saviour of
   mankind.

Bid thou the men, in honour of the greatest of earth's kings

And fortress-owners, fix the nails between his bridle-rings,  1175

With them to bit his charger, that this widely may be
   known,

And all who ride against him may be surely overthrown.

Then in the shock of battle, when the bravest chiefs are
   seeking

To fell their foes beneath the sword, sharp vengeance on
   them wreaking,

He in the fight shall prosper, shall inherit peace victorious,  1180

Who in the front on milk-white steed shall show this bridle  1185
   glorious ;

When warriors famed together rush, swift spears the shield
   assailing,

This weapon in the terror dire will prove a guard unfailing.

Thus did the prophet, wise in thoughts of deepest wisdom,  1190
   sing :

'Known it shall be, that 'neath the brave, the war-horse of
    the king
Shall for its bit and bridle-rings be honoured. And the
    sign
Shall holy be, and he in warlike fame shall ne'er decline    1195
Whom that blest steed shall carry.'" Soon this counsel
    to obey
Bade Helena before the chiefs, adorn without delay
For the great prince, ring-giver of the men, a bridle rare,
And to her son o'er flowing seas she sent the offering fair.
Then all the best and wisest Jews of old heroic race    1200
She bade within the city's bounds assemble in one place;
And there in gentle tones she spake, and taught the lieges    1205
    dear
To love the Lord, and live in peace through all their life-
    days here;
Friendship to keep, and stainless live, their leader's voice
    obeying,—
From Christian deeds, as Cyriacus had taught them, never    1210
    straying.
So stablished was the bishopric. And from afar there
    came
Men weak and feeble in their limbs, the wounded and the
    lame,
The halt, the leprous, and the blind, the lowly and the sad,    1215
And always from the bishop healing found, and freedom
    had

From every woe for ever.  And when to her native land
Return again would Helena, the bishop by her hand          1220
With richest gifts was honoured, while she the people all
Within the realm, both men and maids, who on God's
    name did call,
Bade with their heart and strength and soul to keep that
    day of grace,
On which the holy Rood was drawn from its dark hiding-
    place,
Most famous of the trees that e'er 'neath leafy crown have   1225
    grown
Fair from the earth.   It was the time when spring had
    nearly flown ;
Yet six days more, in May's glad month would dawn the
    summer-tide.
Then closed be hell's dark portal, and heaven's gate thrown
    wide,
And opened be the angels' endless realm, with joys eternal,   1230
There to all those a place be given with Mary, maid
    supernal,
          By whom forgotten never
            Shall be that feast-day high
          Of the dearest Rood that ever
            Was found beneath the sky,               1235
Which the All-Ruler, keeping it from harm,
The Mightiest One, has covered with His arm.

THE END.

#### XV.

\*    \*    \*    \*    \*    \*    \*

IT was thus when age had reached me, and for death I
    ready stood,
In the house where naught I trusted, pondered deeply
    when I could,

Wove the wondrous web of song-craft with the threads my
    wit could keep,
And in night's brief space of silence fed my thought with    1240
    musings deep.

For 'twas little yet I knew about the finding of the Rood,
Until wisdom's heavenly power, which ever has man's
    thought subdued,

Brought to view a wider knowledge.   But, alas! no inward
    peace
Yet was mine, at war with God, by sins enthralled without
    release,

Worn with carking cares and troubles, bitterly by woes
   oppressed,
Till the bounteous King of armies sent to give the old   1245
   man rest,

Learning, ah ! the lasting treasure, in a glorious guise out-
   poured,
Flooding all my mind with clearness, bringing thoughts
   that widely soared,

From all pain released my body, and from woe my bosom   1250
   freeing,
Gave to me the art of song, the joy thenceforward of my
   being

In the world.   Long had I mused already on the glorious
   Tree,
Once, and yet again and often, ere the wonder dawn'd on
   me,

When o'er books and ancient writings long I pored, until   1255
   they told
All the story as it happened, of that mighty Rood of old.


Ne'er till then was aught but sorrow, aught but troubles
   manifold,

Cruel age oppressed the Champion, seas of sorrow o'er
   him rolled,
Yea, though he within the mead-hall treasures took and
   appled gold;

Mourning Yearned sad Need's companion, crushing sorrow  1260
   secret kept,
While his Eagle-wingéd steed the mile-paths measured,
   pranced, and leapt

Proud, with golden trappings.   Ah! life's Winsomeness
   with years has fled;
Vanished is the ancient splendour, youth has faded, joy is  1265
   dead.

Ah! the joy of youth primeval cheering Us in days of
   yore;
Now the years their limit reaching, soon depart, life's joy
   is o'er;
Past it wanders, like the Lake-flood, hurled by tempest
   from the shore.

Fortune 'neath the skies is fleeting; is the land in beauty  1270
   drest,
Soon 'tis gone, as when the wind, beneath the clouds, in
   wild unrest,

Seeks the welkin, raging passes, then all suddenly is
    hushed,
Caged within a narrow prison, and by power oppressed and
    crushed.


Even so this world shall vanish, and all children of her   1275
    born
Shall be seized by flames devouring, when the Lord on
    judgment morn


Comes with all the host of angels.  Then each one who   1280
    words can wield
Shall for every sinful action hear the fitting doom revealed


By the Judge's mouth, and for each word shall pay a
    penalty,
Spoken here in folly, and for thoughts that soared in
    surquedry.


Then shall in three divided be, in grasp of that fierce flame,   1285
All those who ever in all time into the wide earth came.
The men of truth within that fire the uppermost shall be,
All those who thirst for righteousness, a blessed company ;   1290
No heavier their torment than they easily can bear,
The army of the righteous ones.  For them with gracious
    care

The flame shall lose its fervent heat, and with a flickering
    light
Make all their suffering savour less of torment than
    delight.
In middle place are punished they who bear some stain of  1295
    sin,
Men sad at heart, in waves of fire, a cloud of smoke
    within.
In the third part, accursed foes, false tyrants, chained shall
    lie,
Fast in the bottom of the flames, for old iniquity,
In fire's hot grasp the godless throng.   From yonder place
    of pain
Into the gracious mind of God they ne'er shall come again,  1300
Great King of Glory ; but from that fierce furnace shall be
    thrown
Into the pit of hell, to reap the discord they have sown.
Not so the other two.   They shall the God of Hosts  1305
    behold,
The angels' Lord.   From sin set free, and pure as beaten
    gold,
From which in fiery furnace all its dross and every stain  1310
Is wiped away and melted.   So from crimes of deepest
    grain,
And from all sin for ever by the fire of doom made free
Shall be those blessed ones ; and peace eternal theirs  1315
    shall be,

With everlasting weal.    The Angels' Guard, with grace
    excelling
Shall favour them, since every thought and deed of evil
    quelling,
        They ever, in the dust low lying,
        To the Creator's Son were crying.
        Therefore they shall, in fair adorning,
        Shine like the angels of the morning,
        Ever on them from Glory's King descending    1320
        A rich inheritance in time unending.
                          AMEN.

www.ingramcontent.com/pod-product-compliance
Lightning Source LLC
Chambersburg PA
CBHW020313090426
42735CB00009B/1331